Online Dating Success Secrets for Women 40/50+

An "Online dating for Women" Guide

How to find True lasting Love Online

Attract Your Love Hero | Dump the Love Villains

Like I did!

Caryl Westmore

Copyright © 2013 by Caryl Westmore, BA (Hons) EFT and Matrix Reimprinting Trainer (AAMET accredited). Updated 2017.

All rights reserved. No part of this book may be reproduced or transmitted in any form or by any means, electronic or mechanical, without written permission from Caryl Westmore. Inquiries should be addressed to cwestmoreyes@gmail.com

Disclaimer

Please note that Emotional Freedom Techniques - also called EFT Tapping - as recommended in this book are still considered to be in the experimental stages. Caryl Westmore offers these techniques as a personal performance coach and EFT Trainer recognised by the AAMET (Association for the Advancement of Meridian Energy Techniques). She is not a qualified medical professional. Please take full responsibility for your health and emotional well-being.

Book Designer: Bluebobo

Dedication:

This book is dedicated to Nick, my forever soul mate,
best friend and wonderful husband – my true Love Hero.

CONTACT CARYL WESTMORE

FOR YOUR FREE 60-MIN

BREAK FREE TO ATTRACT TRUE SOUL MATE LOVE

Skype coaching session where she will shine a light on your blocks to attracting YOUR Love Hero and lasting forever love.

cwestmoreyes@gmail.com

Skype: breakfreefast

Facebook Messenger:
https://www.facebook.com/CarylWestmore

CONTENTS

PREFACE

KNOW HE'S OUT THERE SOMEWHERE

It's the eternal dream for each of us, to find unconditional true love and acceptance, just as we reached out with expectant hearts and open arms as small children, for others to love and cherish us.

I was over 50 by the time my marriage of 25 years ended in divorce – leaving me feeling like a shipwreck survivor who had been dumped with no resources on the lonely shore of singledom.

Was I scared – you bet!

Dating again seemed an impossibility as I had no social network and no desire to go to pubs and clubs where groups of my age might gather.

Plus I felt over-the-hill, no longer the happy-go-lucky twenty-five-year-old I had been when I married.

Online dating for women my age was unheard of way back in 2000 (unlike today when millions of couples meet online and openly admit it to their friends and family).

But back then I kept it a dark secret, not wanting to admit I needed to "pay" to meet men. There were certainly no books to guide me or help me overcome my fears.

But I threw myself in the deep end and began to apply my passion for self-help topics like The Law of Attraction and later Emotional Freedom Techniques (EFT Tapping) to make it work for me.

It took me seven years of trial and error to build my confidence and my inner "attractor factor" to eventually meet – and marry - my Love Hero.

That's when I began to share my success secrets with other women who begged me to help them.

Now you can benefit from my experience and find love faster and easier using these very same success secrets!

A HAUNTING SONG BY THE MOODY BLUES KEPT ME GOING.

I Know You're Out There Somewhere ran continuously through my heart and mind – and often literally on my stereo – during my years of online dating.

Listen to the song by going to my website: http://carylwestmore .com/truelovesong/ where I have posted a version of it from You Tube. With its haunting melody and lyrics about finding *the one*, "somehow, somewhere", I made it my theme song and promised myself to keep searching, *no matter what!*

Love Eternal will not be denied

As you listen to the song, note the line that seems written for online dating: *"[Some (the naysayers)] Lack the courage and say it's dangerous to try – they just don't know love eternal will not be denied".*

This is exactly what I told myself, believing that we *would* meet – somehow, somewhere – and be together.

I could feel in my heart that my **Love Hero** was out there – seeking me as much as I longed for him. I began to meditate on connecting to him and calling him in across time and space... heart-to-heart. I did that regularly until that's exactly what happened: I met, and later married, my Love Hero, Nick.

So, let this haunting song play in the background of *your* online adventures. *Just know... he is out there somewhere and he'll find **you**, somehow, if you follow my secrets of success.*

Like the song says, "[his] arms will close around you and protect you with the truth".

INTRODUCTION

WHY THIS BOOK IS FOR YOU

Are you over 40 years old, divorced, single and lonely because you believe that true love is beyond your reach?

Are you sick and tired of hoping in vain that Mr. Right will magically appear on the drawbridge of your walled-in heart and rescue you from your castle of loneliness and fear?

Do you have a heart that's been bruised, mangled and trampled on and need some Tender Loving Care from someone who has been there, seen it, done that, and can offer hope, healing and advice? (That's me!)

Then this book is for you!

I promise you that, somewhere out there, is your true lasting love that will make your heart sing.

And your chances of meeting him, wherever he is in the world right now, are far higher when you combine online dating protocols with my success secrets of using energy psychology tool Emotional Freedom Techniques, also called EFT tapping, with the Law of Attraction.

Trust me – I did it, and so can you!

WHY THIS BOOK IS DIFFERENT

How does this book differ from other online dating books?

Firstly, it is written by someone who can relate to your pain because I was once alone and despairing of finding love again because I was over 50. I decided to try online dating because of the encouragement of a friend who was over 40 and who said she had ventured into it successfully.

I hope to be like that friend for YOU.

After my divorce at the age of 50, I overcame my shame and pain I first felt at having to seek a date on the internet. That's when I began to understand that the hidden obstacles to finding love are mainly *within.*

My goal is to share with you the lessons learned from hundreds of hours and dates I spent learning what to do and not do...how to handle the ups and the downs and not lose faith that HE was out there SOMEWHERE!

Eventually it paid off as I beat the odds against time and space to attract and marry my Love Hero.

I will walk you through how it can be done, **step-by-step**.

Secondly, as a coach and trainer, I am expert in helping clients break-free from past pain so they can achieve the **life they love**. I can show you how to successfully apply the tools of EFT Tapping and Law of Attraction, to change your past patterns and beliefs which continue to attract Love Villains. Instead, I'll give you the tools and secrets to magnetize *your* Love Hero.

What I know for sure that much of your history with love and relationships and ongoing challenges inevitably goes back to your early childhood and teen experiences.

Some beliefs and attitudes *can even be tracked back to the womb (how your mother was feeling)* your birth and family of origin. There is evidence that you can inherit certain beliefs from your ancestors, culture, religion and environment – and yes, even from past lives.

It doesn't seem fair that you should be hindered in your destiny to find love now, by the way you experienced love and life in your formative years. But please understand that emotionally intense events, people or traumatic memories, can keep running in your subconscious all your life, and with them, certain core beliefs you carry – like "I'm not loveable or worthy of love".

THE GOOD NEWS IS...

...my expertise and coaching tools can help you source and clear these emotions out, just like erasing malware or a virus from your computer hard-drive – and replacing the damaging beliefs with positive empowering ones. This is the key to dump the pattern of attracting Love Villains – and instead eventually attract your Love Hero.

STEP ONE – DUMP THE "LOVE VILLAINS"

Laugh and cry as you learn to emotionally and energetically **clear out** those Love Villains who lurk in the shadows of your vibrational field. They are a composite of all the nega-tive beliefs, doubts, hurts and fears from **your past**, and they are sabotaging your dream of attracting true love now.

STEP TWO – DEFINE AND CALL IN YOUR "LOVE HERO"

Have fun and get creative as you learn how to apply the Law of Attraction and Intention to **define and magnetize** your Love Hero. Ensure he has all the qualities of romantic love, soul-mate compatibility, caring and sharing that will bring you **lasting happiness** and joy in the partnership of your dreams.

By following these two steps, I found my Love Hero across time and space when I was in Cape Town, South Africa, and he, though from the UK, was working in the Middle East. We met online and within a year were married. Today, 10 years later (2017), we continue to enjoy our passionate, caring and magnetic *forever love* – just as I dreamed it could be.

TO SUM UP

I wrote this book for women over 40 or 50 who want to find new – and true – love, a soul-mate, companionship, sexual joy, happiness and a **second chance at life**. *Like I did!*

This book may also help younger women in their 20s and 30s who are having challenges and heartache with relationship and dating issues. You'd be surprised how many women of that age I have helped steer the course through their love challenges, offline or online, using my suggestions.

Why does it appeal to women of any age?

Because it's based on tried-and-tested principles from my work as a "Break-Free Fast" EFT coach, specializing in helping hundreds of clients find Golden Goal Success with their dreams and goals... especially when it comes to love and fulfilling relationships.

CHAPTER ONE:
TIME TO HEAL THAT BROKEN HEART

In this chapter I am going give you permission to shout from the rooftops, "I've had *enough* of heartache and pain when it comes to men – it's time to heal my broken heart, overcome my fears and **move on!**"

Begin by getting quiet; take some deep breaths and tune into your heart before answering the following questions honestly.

WHERE ARE YOU RIGHT NOW?

Are you shy? Perhaps you are hesitant because you lack dating confidence to put yourself out there?

Are you plagued by self doubt and negative thoughts at the mere mention of it?

Are you a procrastinator? Have you considered signing up for an online dating site, but keep putting it off to "sometime in the future"?

Have you already had your fingers burned and confidence knocked?

Are you one of the lonely, genuinely nice, single women out there who is hurting and fed up with accepting second best – or the booby prize – when it comes to life and love?

Has your heart been battered so badly you are scared of trying again?

Are you puzzled – and in pain – by the way most men have treated you?

Do you see something familiar in this list?

Tell me the truth – have you had ENOUGH and want to change this pattern in your life, starting now?

Make a commitment to yourself – and to me – that you are ready to put a wholehearted effort into changing the course of your love life, starting with this book, and extending to my one-on-one or group coaching sessions to help you break free and succeed online.

My mission is to help you find the fastest route to breaking the seeming curse of being single and lonely.

THERE IS A BETTER WAY

Imagine enjoying flirting, dating, loving again.

Savor the power of choice in dating opportunities. How about several dates in one week with different interesting men – meeting one for coffee in the morning, and another for drinks and dinner in the evening?

Find a lasting and committed relationship with someone who treats you like you deserve to be treated; with intimacy, tenderness, support, respect and when the time is right – fulfilling sexual love.

Picture this: fun, laughter, companionship at the movies or a walk on the beach.

Picture this: yourself on dates with a soul-mate, lover, friend... that special man of your dreams, ideally suited to your interests, education and lifestyle.

Feels terrific, doesn't it?

You can change your lonely life.

If you are single and feeling a bit sorry for yourself, let me reassure you that you can turnaround your fortunes, dramatically increase your chances of dating and mating, and generally live a happy life!

MY OWN TRUE STORY

Everything I share with you in this book I had to learn personally, by trial and error, through many ups and downs. Was my seven-year journey, full of highs and lows, loneliness, despair and experimenting, worth it to share with you the secrets I learnt?

You bet!

This approach, and the healing tools I recommend, gave me back my happiness, confidence, passion and purpose in life. Meeting a fabulous partner was an added bonus that only happened when I began to **love my life**, and dared to wonder, "How can it get any better than this?" as I dreamt of romantic love with someone to share my happiness.

*(Note dear reader, I did **not** say I was looking for someone to **make me happy** – by the time I attracted Nick, I was already pretty happy in my own right.)*

So, not only did this system make me happy, but it also **magnetized Mr. Right** (Nick) into my life – we're still happily married and like baby-boomer honeymooners 10 years later (2017).

This is a miracle when you consider my disastrous track record with one failed 25-year marriage and a rocky road in relationships prior to that. The secret that changed everything is in this book, and I promise to share the exact steps I took to clear the obstacles that were preventing me finding true love, and marriage to the man of my dreams.

I will share with you the best tips and tools, so that you can call in that fabulous Love Hero who is already *looking for you*. Of course, I will also reveal the pitfalls to avoid.

GOOD NEWS: SUCCESS RATES ONLINE

Let me say upfront, I am not promising you an idyllic rose garden. Nor a totally smooth journey to love.

But I can assure you Cupid's arrow works overtime online; thousands of couples fall in love via the internet.

From January 1, 2008 through to June 30, 2009 an average of 542 people were **married every day** in the United States because of the online dating site eHarmony; it created more than 148,311 marriages, or 4.77 percent of all new marriages in the country.

Now, add in all the other successes from the myriad of dating sites available, and you can be confident that you will increase your success rate considerably when you trawl your net in the plentiful fishing waters of online love.

Recent research shows that one in three Americans now meet their spouses online. Best of all, as far as I am concerned, **those marriages are more satisfying and less likely to end in divorce than those that begin in traditional, offline ways.**

Americans are meeting their spouses at work (15 percent), through friends (15 percent), at school (9 percent) or through family (4 percent) less often than in the past, according to a study by Harris Interactive for the period of August 2009 among adults aged 20-54. The study, examining the marital status and satisfaction of 19,131 people who tied the knot between 2005 and 2012, was funded by dating site eHarmony and published in 2013 in the *Proceedings of the National Academy of Sciences* journal.

So you see, you are actually increasing your odds of quality love and marriage by seeking that special Mr. Right on your computer or smartphone app.

Just know for sure, you **can change** your lonely life!

I did it. Several friends who wanted to give up – but after reading this book decided to continue online – also eventually did it!

And so can you. Online. Tonight. *Right now!*

Destiny plays a part in the game of love. But if you apply the suggestions I give you in this book you can do an amazing amount to stack the cards of destiny in your favor.

IS IT SAFE?

Is it safe out there on the internet?

I'd be lying if I said, "Yes, absolutely!"

Like most things in life, ignorance is *not* bliss.

There is a flipside to the rosy picture I have painted. Rather than being scary, facing up to the flipside from the start will empower you and ensure you are committed to putting yourself, and your **intuitive feelings**, first.

Flipside Men are weirdoes, married, separated, liars, selfish, addicts of some kind (gambling, drinks, drugs, work,) or casa nova charmers with no intention of settling down. In other words, the archetypal **Love Villain**. These men are looking for women with all the attributes of their immature fantasies – great looks, hot bodies, mind-blowing sex – while some are on the hunt for gullible women with money.

The Love Villain is a composite of all your worst experiences, but I'll teach you how to define and delete him from your energy field. Instead you'll discover how to create a picture of your **Love Hero** to call into your reality through the secrets of the Law of Attraction and the power of intention.

CASE STUDY: PATRICIA

I started this book after numerous friends asked me to tell them how I did it, so they could pass on some tips to their single friends.

An example is a friend in my book club who I will call Patricia (not her real name). She was forlorn after yet another heart break: "Marty and I were on the brink of marriage when his ex came back into the picture and he didn't have the strength to stand up to her. Online dating sucks – this is the third time I've felt dumped...I'm giving up for good!" she said.

"Don't give up," I advised, "Read my book (I sent her a first draft) and give it one more go."

Six months later, she looked radiant and left the book club to focus on golfing with her new man. Today she is happily married to him.

THE UPSIDE OF ONLINE DATING

10 GOOD REASONS TO GIVE ONLINE DATING A GO

1. You can meet someone new in the privacy of your own home, without agonizing about where to go to meet other like-minded singles.
2. You can mix and mingle solo, without having to drag along a friend for moral support.
3. You can ignore that zit or the dark roots that need a touch-up.
4. You can chat to someone without putting on your make up or dressing up to the nines.
5. You can meet someone really interesting in a completely different circle of people from those you already know; or in a different part of town, city or country.

6. The costs are minimal. The price of a one-month contract on a dating site is about the same as a meal out with a glass of wine. You can register free on most sites to test the water by taking a look at other profiles. (Be aware that you need to pay before you can contact or respond to anyone – the sites are businesses after all.)

7. You can avoid the shame of your friends fixing you up with a terrible blind date just because he or she knows someone single.

8. You need no longer be tempted to date, or have a fling with, a co-worker or, worse, your boss.

9. There is less random luck involved than just waiting for Fate to strike.

10. You can increase your chances of meeting the right person by emailing or responding to more than one potential love match at a time.

AFFIRMATION:

"Online dating means you never have to feel abandoned, sorry for yourself or stay home alone."

MY INTENTIONS FOR YOU WITH THIS BOOK:

- I want *you* to feel good and enjoy life again.
- Give online dating a go without feeling like a failure if you don't immediately find your fairy tale ending.
- Save you the needless pain, ignorance and heartache that many women go through when starting out online dating.
- Benefit from practical tools and tips that can make all the difference to your success.

YOU WILL LEARN:

- How to get crystal clear about what you want out of the online dating experience.
- How to set your intention for the experience you desire to have.
- How to decide what you *do not* want in a date and future relationship.
- How to magnetize what you *do* want in a date and future relationship.
- What *not* to say in a profile.
- What *to* say in a profile to attract your Love Hero.
- How soon to arrange to meet in person.
- Follow up protocol.
- How to respond when he's just not into you.

TO SUM UP

So there you have it – if you give online dating a go, approaching it with the tools and tips I spent years testing and mastering, you too can start enjoying *forever love*, sooner than you think!

CHAPTER TWO:
LAW OF ATTRACTION LOVE SECRETS

In this chapter I am going to reveal my own special recipe for love success, which I developed during my online dating adventures.

It's based on the **Law of Attraction** formula as explained by the teachings of Abraham Hicks and popularized in the movie *The Secret*, but also uses tips on realizing your dreams from a book called ***The Cosmic Ordering Service***, by Barbel Mohr.

COSMIC ORDERING

I like Mohr's description of a "Cosmic male ordering service" as follows.

She started with a nine-item wish list for the perfect man, which included that he be:

- vegetarian;
- against alcohol;
- a non-smoker;
- a lover of Tai Chi

She even set an exact date – three months ahead – for delivery.

When the set date arrived, a guy with all the requisite characteristics was promptly delivered. But Mohr decided she wanted an improved version. So she created a new order with a 15-item list. When this was also not entirely accurate enough, she expanded the list to 25 items. Eventually she met and married her perfect Love Hero.

According to Mohr: "Cosmic ordering means asking the whole of creation for help when you have a problem you can't solve yourself. I call it the Cosmos, but you could call it God, Creation, your guardian angel, Allah, your higher self – or whatever form of address you feel most comfortable with." She explains that the Cosmos hears and reacts to the messages that we send out – it is then just up to us to watch out for the answers.

She believes that love is an "inside job", meaning that you have to feel you deserve and are worthy of receiving the goods you ordered (your perfect Love Hero). It means having a deep certainty that you are ready to give to, and receive love from, your dream soul-mate.

How *you* feel about you, is far more important than who you meet or how much you weigh. When you value and love yourself, you can listen to the opportunities, nudges and prompts that tell you what is right for *you*, your inner state creates and magnetizes your reality.

But when we are stressed, under pressure, feeling angry or unworthy, we send a mixed message of "not good enough" with our requests – bingo, the Cosmos delivers mixed results!

THE LAW OF ATTRACTION

The Law of Attraction, as described in the movie *The Secret*, is about creating your life by attracting whatever you think about, feel and focus your attention on, whether consciously or unconsciously.

So, saying things like, "I have such bad luck with men", or, "all the good men are taken at my age", plants the seed for that reality to manifest in your life. Your subconscious, the Universe and the Cosmic Ordering Service receive your exact wording and cancel out any other orders you had previously listed for your Love Hero.

This is beautifully summed up by the genie from Aladdin's magic lamp in *The Secret*, saying, "Your wish is my command", as well as the story related in the movie by acclaimed Feng Shui expert Marie Diamond.

Feng Shui is the ancient Chinese art of energy and placement, and Marie described how she was once called in to consult with a good-looking film producer in Los Angeles whose hobby was painting. On entering his home she took one look at his paintings and said she would bet that he was having trouble in his romantic life. She was spot on. He confided that despite being surrounded by hundreds of beautiful single women and available actresses, he never dated.

Diamond had spotted that the paintings displayed in his home all showed a woman with a haughty expression, tossing him a look of disdain over her shoulder. "You are getting the exact result of this image," Diamond told the amazed film producer. "Change the attitude of the women you paint into scenes of romantic love."

Soon he reported that he was flooded with offers from a multitude of women and was enjoying dating them all. Months later, he complained, "Now I'm tired of dating so many women. I want to fall madly in love and settle down with one special woman." "Then paint it," replied Diamond. Within a year he reported that he had met and married the woman of his dreams.

The same can happen to you. In Chapter 4 I will show you exactly how to create a vivid picture of the kind of Love Hero you want to attract – in both words and pictures – and how to fire it up with imagination and feelings.

But first let's look at the part your **beliefs** play in all of this.

In her book, *Travelling Free...How To Recover From The Past By Changing Your Beliefs*, Mandy Evans lists 20 self-defeating beliefs. They include what I describe as the "Top Five Love Killer Beliefs" that will prevent you attracting true love with the Law of Attraction.

TOP FIVE LOVE KILLER BELIEFS

If any of the following self-defeating beliefs apply to you, it could be ruining your chances of love, on or offline.

1. **I'm not good enough to be loved**
   You may not say it, or even know you believe this deep down, but you could be stuck with this very common belief if you have had family and friends commiserate with you for how badly men have treated you.

2. **I am not a success in life without the romantic love-of-my-life**
   There's a book by Penelope Russianoff with a title that says it all: *Why do I think I am nothing without a man?* Irish writer Claudia Carroll penned a hilarious novel, *Remind Me Again Why I Need a Man*, which answers that question through the story of Amelia Lockwood who only ever wanted to get married – "the Tiffany ring, the Vera Wang dress...the whole shebang." Women for whom this fallacy seems true fail to enjoy the other wonders in life: friendships, family, the glory of nature, or the pride and pleasure of mastering new challenges mean nothing as long as she is not romantically involved.

3. **Love is Scarce**
   This myth causes women to latch on and hold tight at the first hint of a budding relationship. They do not have relationships, they take hostages who finally break free, leaving them sure they must hold on even tighter next time!

4. **Rejection is too painful and must be avoided at all costs.** This belief limits the ability to explore any relationship to the full. Avoiding rejection at all costs actually stunts relationships from growing in intimacy and strength. Each heartbreak I had on my journey of online dating expanded my capacity to love and understand my own feelings better.

5. **Failure means I wasted my love on him (and should give up)** Watch out for this one in the game of online dating. If you ask for guarantees too soon, you can cripple chances of a seed of love growing and flourishing in its own good time. If you invest yourself in a relationship for some length of time (especially if you live in a different town or country and rely on email, phone or Skype) and it goes belly-up, you have two choices: Get stuck in a circle of deep hurt, self-hatred and blame;

or

Reframe it as a "growth experience" and move on.
It may be a cliché, but it really works to remind yourself, "better to have loved and lost than never to have loved at all". Provided, of course, you clear the inner beliefs that you spot as playing a part in sabotaging the love!

CASE STUDY: FOOL FOR LOVE

For two months I built up a great email and telephone friendship with Paul (69). We shared a love of classical music, nature, animals and so much more – we were we both smitten and couldn't wait to meet each other in person. I was hesitant to believe we could really fall in love so fast, but he told me, "just let yourself fall".

The challenge was that we lived hundreds of miles away and he could not leave his seven-month-old St Bernard puppy on its own. So, as he lived alone on a beautiful nature estate in the country, he suggested I visit him.

Paul agreed to first put me up in a luxury hotel not far from his home, where we could get to know each other before I made the move to his estate. He treated me like a queen, but things were not all as they seemed to be...

He hadn't thought to tell me he was on medication for severe depression after a breakdown and I noticed he was compulsive obsessive about the way things needed to be. He was a typical Howard Hughes millionaire recluse with some decidedly eccentric behavior.

In fact the magic chemistry was missing for both of us when we actually got to know each other in person, and when I left to go home, we were both quietly relieved. But my trust in myself was shattered.

How could I have been so hoodwinked by him – and, more importantly, by my own dream fantasy? Everything had turned out to be an illusion.

I began to question my worth; whether I should just give up and resign myself to being alone. I swore off dating for several months. I vowed I would never be so naïve again, but I stopped myself from becoming bitter or feeling sorry for myself.

I made a Gratitude List that included:

I was grateful that, even if only for a brief time, I had been treated like a queen. It felt good – Universe, bring on more of that please!

I was grateful that I could forgive myself for being a "fool for love" and move on.

Finally I was grateful that I could affirm wholeheartedly: "I choose to treat myself with love and respect and expect the same from the Love Hero who I can vividly imagine one day coming into my life."

TO SUM UP

In this chapter I have introduced the magnetic recipe for love success – using the Law of Attraction and/or the Cosmic Male Ordering Service to visualize and magnetize your Love Hero.

I have warned you about several of many self-defeating beliefs that you must heal. At the end of the day, love is an inside job and the more you love yourself, the better your chances are of calling in your Love Hero.

Use your online dating experiences to grow wiser and mindful of what's right for you – while opening your heart to life and not allowing disappointment to mar your happiness.

This is ultimately the path to living happily ever after when you do meet your Love Hero.

CHAPTER THREE:
LOVE VILLAINS: WHAT YOU DON'T WANT

In this chapter I am going to help you focus on what you don't want, in order to free up your mind to conjure up an image of what you do want. But let's not jump the gun just yet, we need to get rid of the Love Villain first and I will introduce you to two methods that have worked for me, my friends and clients.

THE LOVE VILLAIN

You're about to come face-to-face with the man I refer to as the Love Villain. He's a nightmare composite of all the worst characteristics of all the men you've ever encountered, dated or had a relationship with - who inevitably broke your heart or left you feeling abandoned, miserable or demeaned.

But the good news is, I'll also give you the magic tools to disentangle your heart-strings from wanting him – or men like him – and show you how to eradicate the Love Villain's shadowy influence from your love life, so you can break free, finally, to attract and call in your Love Hero.

LOOKING BACK

Even before you decided to venture into online dating you probably encountered your share of painful *unwanted* experiences. Rather than cringing away from the experiences, use them to look for clues for the origins of your Love Villain:

Ever since your teenage years, when you first fell in love or felt unworthy of love, you have accumulated a variety of trapped emotions associated with love. These past partners can help you unravel the source of your Love Villain.

Your childhood home and parental influence will also affect your views on love to this day; the interactions between your parents, how they treated you and your siblings, plus moments of intensity in your early life, have all resulted in your beliefs and how you feel about yourself today. For some of my clients, bullying or abusive siblings destroyed their belief in themselves and enabled them to be victims of shabby treatment from men in adult life.

There are two ways to find the original imprint of the Love Villain:

- Method 1: a current love crisis or heartbreak; or
- Method 2: tracing a timeline.

THE REMEDY

In both cases, the most powerful way I recommend you begin the clearing is to book a session with a coach who uses Emotional Freedom Techniques (EFT Tapping) – which is like psychological acupuncture – together with EFT advanced protocol Matrix Reimprinting. That way, you will combine the clearing with reimprinting positive empowering new beliefs and memories, all in one session.

As this is my specialty, you may want to book a FREE 15 minute

Discovery Session with me by emailing cwestmoreyes@gmail.com or by contacting me on Skype **@breakfreefast.**

You can find a video explanation of How To Tap at http://carylwest more.com/eft-tapping/ and there is lots more information in my books *You Can Break Free Fast (EFT Tapping)* and *Goal Success (EFT Tapping)*, which are available on Amazon.

METHOD 1: CURRENT CRISIS

WHEN A LOVE TRAUMA HAPPENS

When you have a specific love trauma that knocks you for six – like a lover dumped you without any reason and it brings up feelings of abandonment – it's a perfect time to get going with EFT tapping and Matrix Reimprinting. It will help you get through the shock, bewilderment and pain immediately, as well as preventing these unhealed wounds from affecting your future chances of finding love.

If thoughts of your ex are all-consuming and you feel like you'll never get over him, then I can almost guarantee the break-up has triggered a past trauma (and resulting beliefs) going way back, possibly even as far as your early childhood.

The good news is that once we support and release that Younger You, the Adult You will miraculously heal.

YOUR PART IN THIS MANIFESTATION

You have to accept that you – or rather that younger you – subconsciously manifested the experience into your life. If this sounds crazy, I'll show you how it works.

When devastating or hurtful dating experiences happened to me I stopped and asked myself: "What part of me still believes, resonates with or reflects this kind of behavior?" I considered that I might still be vibrating a belief, thought or feeling within me that actually mirrored the outward treatment I received.

In other words, if part of me – at a subconscious level – is fearful of commitment or believes I am not worthy of love, then I will subconsciously recreate situations that prove this is true.

You could also call it the Law of Attraction or Resonance – your inner vibration is sending out signals like a radio station that manifest in the treatment you are getting.

TAPPING FOR CLUES

This is the cue to start slow tapping until you are in tune with your body enough to ask as you tap: "When have I felt like this before?"

You are tapping on a feeling which has been triggered by a current event, but which can be traced back through the years – from memory to memory – until you source the feeling, sometime before the age of six.

I usually begin with: "When did you feel like that most recently? Tell me about an incident which brought up similar feelings (of pain/outrage/anger etc)."

At this point I would introduce Matrix Reimprinting with the EFT tapping, whereby we step into the memory and address our Younger Self or ECHO (Energy Consciousness Hologram). We ask her how she is feeling and then continue the dialogue with tapping to release the trauma aspects of what she is going through.

This is likely take you back to an even earlier experience. When you find this event, you can tap on and dialogue with that even younger self "in the matrix". Then, when she feels whole, you find another even earlier part of you, until you eventually source the originating seed that is vibrating this kind of experience.

An example could be an important figure in your childhood dying or leaving unexpectedly... like your father suddenly abandoning the family and later divorcing your mother; or your beloved older brother being sent away to boarding school. In some cases, clients have lost a mother or sister and have projected the deep feelings of loss and abandonment associated with that, onto the current relationship ending.

BREAKING THE TREND

Every traumatic experience involving relationships will leave you with a belief, feeling or vibration that the situation is how things should be. When you believe that, you will attract more of it into your life.

Use this current unhappy experience as the gateway to create what *you want* instead. That is how you get back your power and start to create happier experiences in the future.

Remember: feelings buried alive from your past never die, but lie dormant waiting for the next trigger that activates an emotional response from you.

You will find **a recognizable pattern in your past**, a pattern that may make you sick to your core when you realize that you've been replaying it endlessly in your relationships.

Please note: if you do unearth some deeply disturbing feelings, then please seek professional help and support. It's important to reach out for help when you need it and not drowning on your own.

CASE STUDY EXAMPLE: NICKY

Nicky was an attractive, slim, brunette of 35 with a successful job in retail marketing, but she came to me frustrated about her inability to sustain even one long-term relationship in her adult life. Somehow she had always attracted men who lied to her or let her down.

"It's winter," she says, "and all my friends are nesting with their mates – I'm overwhelmed with frustration and longing for my own relationship. What's keeping me stuck alone and single?"

The EFT tapping session began with a set up phrase around her feelings and belief: "I am not good enough to win at love."

She estimated it was at a level of **9 out of 10**.

As we tapped on the Karate Point she repeated:

Even though I'm not good enough to win at love, I love and accept myself anyway;

Even though I don't have a clue why men let me down, I choose to love and accept myself anyway; and

Even though I'm feeling alone and doomed to be single forever, I now choose to release this pattern and find a new way.

Nicky proceeded to tap on the points with reminder phrases like:

Not good enough;

My sisters said so;

I'm not like them (smaller and different);

Different from my family;

Different from my friends;

They all bond together and love each other; and

Why doesn't anyone love *me*?

She paused for a minute and corrected herself...

"Well that's not entirely true – my two aunts loved me and spoiled me."

As we continued the session, Nicky revealed that she had always admired and felt connected to her two single aunts Sally and Sandy. Somehow they seemed freer, happier and more successful than her mother who was a stay-at-home-mom, focused on her husband and family.

During this formative time she made a decision that she was the outsider in her family and identified strongly with her two single aunts.

It was if she had made a vow to be like them – but the cost far outweighed the benefits because it made her *subconsciously* shy away from men who might "tie her down" in a marriage like her mother.

Dean was her most recent disappointment... before that was Oliver, who she had moved cities to be with, leaving her friends and network behind; it ended badly, as he just wanted to be friends.

But earlier than that, aged 17 her first love Craig lied and cheated on her, leaving her with a belief that all men are cheaters or unattainable.

We tracked this back using EFT tapping to her earlier childhood where the feelings of low self-worth originated. Her Younger Self felt she would be safer and happier pursuing a successful career as a single woman.

Nicky realized that unless she cleared these old beliefs and patterns, she would continue to be a prisoner.

In just one session, we were able to help Nicky release her biggest inner belief obstacles to love, and to reimprint new empowering messages such as:

I *am worthy* of love and total acceptance;

I now release the need to act as an outsider when it comes to love and life; and

I embrace my life fully in wholeness and joy, and open myself to love and marriage, while still being a success in my work.

Nicky left her session feeling like a new woman. A few months later she reported that she had met a wonderful new love, and within a year they had announced their engagement and plans for marriage.

BREAK FREE FAST

After more than 20 years helping clients to "break free fast" using emotional-energy tools like The Journey, EFT tapping (Emotional Freedom Techniques) and Matrix Reimprinting, I know for sure that these techniques are key in helping you source and root out these toxic love patterns and emotions.

That means putting a stop to unconscious repetitive behavior and faulty childhood beliefs of guilt, shame and pain, which can be running and ruining your life – and chances for love – now.

The time has come to release co-dependent behavior, liberating you to have a second chance at life and love. Two authors have influenced me in understanding this so fully, and helped me prepare the exercises for you below: Harville Hendrix's insights on Imago Therapy as outlined in his book *Getting the Love You Find*; and Barbara de Angelis in her book *Are You the One for Me?*

METHOD 2: THE TIMELINE

Take a blank sheet of paper – or your journal – and write down the following:

- List the names of all the men who you've been emotionally involved with, attached to, or had meaningful relationships with;
- After each name, make a list of their most **negative qualities** – a word or two rather than long sentences, for example *moody, depressed, unfaithful, critical;*
- Circle all the qualities that repeat themselves from one person to the next;
- Make a summary list; and
- Review the meaning that has surfaced.

CASE STUDY: REPETITIVE PATTERNS

My friend Susan noticed a pattern of the "**eternal triangle**" repeating itself in her life story. She was shocked to notice that all her major love interests involved some kind of entanglement with another woman waiting in the wings.

In my life I seemed to attract men who didn't show their anger or disapproval, but instead sulked silently and caused *me* to boil over with anger. Their unexpressed aggression drove me into outbursts of anger leaving me feeling alienated, while they retreated to lick their wounds. When my anger subsided, I would feel guilty.

I eventually found that this originated from a pattern in my early childhood home: my mother was a saintly woman who silently suffered my father's emotional outbursts when he had too much to drink, nightly. I was playing it out in my relationships, switching roles with my father in the game of angry vs. silent and passive sufferer.

Once I had my *AHA!* moment, I found I could change my subconscious programming.

NOW IT'S YOUR TURN

WANTED: LOVE VILLAIN ADVERT

The Law of Attraction and Cosmic Ordering Service show that you get what you ask for, so you have to recognize that you have been requesting – and receiving – your Love Villains. So let's try writing an over-the-top imaginary profile for a dating site stipulating all the worst negative traits you unearthed above.

Mine might have read:

WANTED

A moody, brilliant passive-aggressive man to keep me anxious and nervous about never getting it right to help make him feel better, no matter how hard I try. Only victims with chronically abusive childhoods need apply because my job will be to mother, control and do my best to convince you of my love and support. When I fail, you will blame me and I will beat up myself. You must have a hopeless Peter Pan attitude to money and success to add to my insecurity, nagging and unhappiness. Also welcome are your chronic addictions around smoking, alcohol or drugs, and my powerlessness to reform you!

Or take my client Tessa's ad:

WANTED

Charming, lazy man for a demeaning relationship that leaves me feeling exhausted. I'm looking for someone whose idea of a good weekend is to glue himself to the couch, down beers and smoke while watching sport on television. Better still if your mates can join you to watch the big match. And then you all go off to celebrate, leaving me to clean up the empty cans and overflowing ash trays. Chronic lateness and lying are pluses.

WHAT I DON'T WANT

Take some time to answer the following questions to help you identify what you don't want out of a relationship.

- What is currently making me unhappy?
- How am I betraying myself right now?
- How am I playing small in my love life?
- What has been my lowest point in the past month? How did it make me feel?
- What do you have to believe about yourself to create this situation in your love life?
- What is the thing you are most afraid to say out loud about your love life?

Now take time to write your NOT-WANTED AD.

LAUGH UNTIL IT HURTS

Take the mickey out of yourself, as hard as it might be. Make it outrageous, ridiculous, and hopelessly hilarious.

Why?

It's okay to make fun of yourself and your past choices, because:

You don't want to repeat them again – when you see them coming, you can stop the rush of attraction and shout, "No!" much earlier on in the relationship; and

Once you wake up from the trance you've been in, you're free to make new choices. And there's nowhere better to start than on the internet.

HEAL YOUR "INNER CHILD"

Your Inner Child has been running the emotional show. She is the one who feels "at home" with a man who reminds her of her mother, father, sibling, or the significant care-giver who most influenced her earliest years. She is the one who feels too helpless to leave when all the signs point to being crazy to put up with the treatment you are getting.

Do the inner clearing work in this chapter and you give yourself a far better chance of success in finding a lasting and happy relationship... online, or anywhere else for that matter.

I've helped hundreds of people over the past 20 years as a Journey Therapist and EFT-Matrix Reimprinting Practitioner, focusing on helping clients heal past "inner child" pain.

Once you really get it – that the Adult You is no longer as helpless and vulnerable as the Inner Child you once were – your future suddenly opens to all-new possibilities.

The Adult You can release the emotional glitches and beliefs that were set in place by the toxic behavior (thoughtlessness, cruelty, addiction, grief-stricken and self-involvement) of your mother, father, siblings, or other care-givers.

Our thoughts, feelings and internal belief system all play a much more powerful part in attracting "Forever Love" than we realize. It's usually only when things go wrong and we collapse, hurt and bleeding in a heap of pain, that we seek help.

TO SUM UP

In this chapter I showed you why and how to break free from the past – going back to resolve childhood influences that are causing you problems now.

I explained how energy psychology tools, EFT tapping with Matrix Reimprinting, can source and release damaging influences.

I have shown you the vital importance of identifying **What You Don't Want**, before going on to the fun part –dreaming **What You Do Want**.

CHAPTER FOUR:
LOVE HERO: DREAM WHAT YOU DO WANT

It's your life, your destiny. What are the best qualities you want in a man?

In this chapter I reveal some potent secrets to "dream your Love Hero into reality".

You're going to have to specify your preferences when you register on a dating site, so my advice is to do it long before you go online.

Don't wait until you are faced with the list one lonely night and get confused by the questions. The multiple-choice questions take time and make you think about yourself, but they can be distracting and confuse you over what is *important to you* in a relationship.

Get cracking as soon as you have completed the "what I don't want" exercises and cleared emotional clutter from the past.

Be clear on the menu of your deepest wishes and desires for the man of your dreams, and stipulate it to the Universe.

Or rather, let's use the word "preferences." Realize that you may *prefer* a tall man who looks like George Clooney, but end up with a shorter, balding man who lights your fire because he is kind, humorous, honest... and sparks the special chemistry that you stipulated on your *wants* list.

NOTE HOW IT BEGINS

I believe in something I heard from Barefoot Doctor, the UK's famous Tao healing expert and author who I worked with some years ago.

"How a relationship begins foretells how it will continue," he said. And I think he's right.

Each encounter has its unique beginning, but online dating has two portentous moments; first as you start internet dating and, then again, when you first meet.

Does he open the door and pay for the coffee and movie – or does he stand back and expect you to pay half of everything from the minute you meet?

Does he hide from your view and watch you from a distance at the venue you have chosen to meet? And then step forward, presumably when he has decided whether or not he likes the look of you?

CASE STUDY: MEAN MAX

The meanest man I ever met was Max. Our first date was at a coffee shop in a shopping mall and he made sure I paid for half the bill.

Now, I am not saying the man must always pay, but it was only a few bucks and I thought, if he can't reach for the bill for coffee, then how generous would he be in other areas, such as sharing his time or love?

Also on that first date, he said, "To this day I hate my mother and will happily dance on her grave when the time comes," which raised a red flag. Just as you or I may carry unresolved issues about men going back to early childhood (which I urge you to clear with EFT-Matrix Reimprinting), I would be very wary of getting involved with a man so angry towards his mother!

As it turned out, many months later I discovered by chance some very *unsavory* things about Max, which backed up my gut feeling at the time.

LOVE MAPPING

Love-mapping is like mind-mapping, or brain-storming, from the heart.

I recommend you do it with a companion or girlfriend because it makes it so much more fun. It's also helpful for expanding your list of wants, and getting valuable insights, as you share and comment on each other's disasters – and dreams.

MY EXPERIENCE

I joined forces with my single friend Helen once and she, being a creative executive in advertising, got out her flip chart – and a glass of wine – to encourage our brainstorming and love-mapping.

We laughed, we cried, we sighed: we listed our **wants** and **not-wants** in men.

We honed in first on our worst nightmare partners. Like her fiancé who snooped on her computer when she was out, even accessing her bank accounts. Or her pattern for attracting men who already had wives or partners; "eternal triangles".

I shared my distaste for dishonesty and lies. Like the man who, after weeks of dating, suddenly did not turn up to collect me for a movie date as he had left the country – he clearly thought nothing of how this would affect me emotionally, which began with making frantic calls to the police and hospitals in case he had been in a car accident, or worse.

By the end of the afternoon Helen and I had emptied out our worst dating memories and made an extensive list of what the *opposite* of these might be in an ideal relationship with our dream man. Using the notes on the flip chart, I got a long list of my most wanted characteristics in a partner. Later I transferred this to my journal and made a **collage with words and pictures** of my **Love Hero** and **ideal relationship**.

This gave me the outline and details for my online profile and soon, in Chapter 5, I will share with you how to write a winning online profile.

For now I suggest you focus on what you *do want*, so that you are crystal clear about your desires and intention when it comes to "calling in the one".

REFRAME AND RAISE YOUR EXPECTATIONS

It takes courage to test the waters and dive into the world of online dating at first, and no doubt you will have some downs as well as ups. But you can learn from all experiences.

I believe that if you use all events – the good, bad or indifferent – as part of your growth, doing what is called "re-framing" in Neuro Linguistic Programming, then you are gearing yourself for success.

Re-framing is changing the meaning of an experience or an event by putting another "frame" around it. It's seeing an **opportunity** (not a problem), or giving a new interpretation of **empowering** (rather than disabling) to whatever happens to you.

Instead of crawling into a hole and beating yourself up because a date you thought had potential never contacted you again, **stop and reframe**. Stop telling yourself it was because you are "too fat" or "talked too much." Just tell yourself... "Next!"

Raising your self-value is key.

It has been proven time and time again that **self-esteem** plays a major role in **success**. Do you want to come across as an Eeyore, the pessimistic donkey in Winnie the Pooh, fearing the worst as you try internet dating, focusing on what could go wrong?

Instead, picture yourself as Tinkerbell from Peter Pan; a "creature unlike any other" with a voice like a tinkling bell and the invitation to sprinkle pixie dust to make you fly into wonderful online dating adventures in the land of your dreams.

CASE STUDY: REFRAME ME

After my divorce, I started out carrying far too much weight, both literally and emotionally. The unprocessed baggage and unwanted kilograms came with a very low level of self-worth and expectation. But as time went on, my self-worth and dating "fitness" improved.

I began to raise the bar of my expectations and dreams, bit by bit, date by date. I lost weight, went to yoga and joined a hiking club. But I was doing that for me as much as to become my alter ego, the sexy siren Marvella (my online dating profile pseudonym).

I also did tons of self-work to clear the past and heal my inner child, which you can do with EFT-Matrix Reimprinting

Gradually a laughing, likeable, spontaneous side of me emerged from the damaged, prickly, angry, shell I had become. In time I grew happier, healthier and more self-confident – someone I rather enjoyed being with – and so my relationships improved.

CREATE A GREAT LOVE FUTURE NOW

Try this exercise to help imagine your perfect future and clarify your desires for your Love Hero.

1. Imagine it's a year in the future and you have had the best year of your dating life, thanks to your courage of going online.

- What has happened in your love life that made your heart sing, boosted your confidence sky-high
- What wonderful experiences do you have of your romance journey?
- Who have you met that was significant?
- Where have you made significant progress?
- What are your big wins?
- What behaviors did you practice?
- Who are you becoming that makes you feel good about yourself?

2. Now make an ideal scene – movie-like – of you looking positive and happy, a smile on your face and love vibration all around. Make the feeling you get either realistic or symbolic – you having confetti and rose petals thrown over you on your wedding day, or just you jumping for joy saying, "Yes, Yes, Yes!"

3. Take that image and put it into your timeline one year in the future. Make sure the image is really big, bold, colorful and vivid. You'll feel really terrific doing this.

4. Now chunk your timeline backwards in smaller steps. Make a slightly smaller picture and place it a few months before the big picture.

    What will need to happen before that? How have your months of dating this wonderful man culminated with him getting down on one knee and proposing?

    Now make an even smaller picture and place it a few months before the last image. Perhaps you have revamped your body by losing 20kg and look lean and energetic, or your internet date wined and dined you one magical night when you somehow both realized your searches were over.

Keep doing the chunking, step by step, backwards month by month, between then and now.

You now have a succession of pictures connecting the present with your positive, compelling future. The images should get progressively bigger and brighter, with more exciting things happening to you in them.

5. Look at these pictures and let your unconscious mind soak in the road map that you have created on your Timeline – use every sense sight, taste, smell, touch and sound.

6. Now float up out of your body and into each picture, step-by-step, fully feeling the experience of the various stages of your progress in each picture.

7. When you get to the big picture of your Ultimate Outcome – showered with confetti and rose petals, a shining ring on your finger and heart bursting with love and happiness – then really amp it up to maximum intensity. What will it feel like to have your dreams come true in love? What will it be like to have everything you want?

8. Finally come back to the present and look ahead along your future Timeline. You can feel confident in the knowledge that you have created a map of love along a visionary route. And your Magic Genie has watched the intense feelings of gusto you felt about it and pronounces: **"Your Wish is My Command!"**

TO SUM UP

In this chapter you had the fun task of using your imagination to create your **Love Hero** in vivid detail, and to imagine your future with him already in your life.

CHAPTER FIVE:
BUILD A WINNING PROFILE

In this chapter I share the top Dos and Don'ts of making that first impression count when it comes to your Profile and Picture.

Men browsing the dating sites will flip through hundreds of profiles. You have just **20 seconds** to impress. What can *you* do to stand out with the *wow* factor?

Many dating sites have questionnaires designed to help new customers fill in their profile, and by all means start with those. But please take heed of the tips in this chapter to create *your* winning profile.

HOW ARE YOU FEELING?

Pay attention to how you are feeling when you sit down to write your profile – never approach this task when you're feeling low, desperate or negative about yourself, dating or life in general!

Prepare your heart and mind by doing a round of EFT Tapping; make sure you clear out any self-doubt and criticism, and **tap into positive empowering words and feelings**.

EFT Tapping script examples: *for writing profile*

- Even though I'm feeling scared of rejection, I deeply and profoundly love and accept myself anyway;
- Even though I don't know how to "sell myself", I can choose to do it playfully; and
- Even though it feels a bit painful doing this to meet someone, I can choose to give it my best shot... and who knows, like thousands of others, I can fine true love online!

Do this first and you'll approach the task feeling inspired, hopeful and upbeat, having allowed your innermost fears to be released through tapping.

For your profile, set your intention to put your best side forward, if possible with a light-hearted humorous touch.

PART 1: THE PROFILE WORDING

HOW LONG SHOULD IT BE?

Make your profile about 300 words.

Of these, 250 words will be about *you* and 50 words about your *ideal match*.

Be brief enough to **pique interest**. It's been proven that men look at photos first and then skim the information in your profile. Remember you have just **20 seconds.**

Avoid clever, sarcastic short profiles that say: "If you want to know more, just ask me."

Why? Because it lacks the "attraction factor" that you want to infuse into your winning profile.

SIX TOP TIPS TO SPARKLE

Pretend you're talking to a new person at a cocktail party, and you're telling him about what you do, if you have family etc.

1. Mention your career; past, present and aspirations for the future.

2. If you have children or grandchildren, say so – after all, this is an important part of your life

3. If you speak a foreign language – or have lived or travelled to interesting countries – describe this because it's a good ice-breaker online. You may have done a cooking class when you visited Morocco, a yoga course in Spain or photography in New York; paint a picture and entice them in.

4. If you're new to a town or country where you'd like to make new friends, say so – even if romance doesn't blossom, you may find people who will help you settle in and give welcome advice.

5. Talk about your hobbies and interests like bridge, music or golf. Describe specific details that will spark the imagination and invite a response to your profile, such as any tournaments you are in, venues you have been to or pieces you have exhibited.

6. When it comes to the 50 words to describe your ideal match, saying what you don't want is fine – like smoking – but try to rephrase it in a nicer way: "Would love someone who is health-conscious and doesn't smoke – fancy coming to the gym with

me or planning ski trips together?" Don't be shy to say "looking for a stable relationship" if that's your heart's desire.

SIX TOP TIPS TO AVOID (AT ALL COSTS)

1. Don't add touches of anger, sarcasm or hurt carried over from the past.

2. Don't talk about previous relationships **at all** in your profile.

3. Don't under-estimate the importance of a great photo (see later) – your picture must be clear, accurate, eye-catching and high quality.

4. Don't be sexually suggestive – unless you are focusing on a site specifically with that in mind.

5. Don't be corny or clichéd, using catchphrases or tag lines that many other profiles use like: "I might be the one you are look-ing for". Do some research before writing your profile and note what phrases and wording are over-used. Then avoid them!

6. Don't be too general, avoid using vague adjectives in your ad like: "I am honest, spontaneous, creative, and intuitive". Instead, define yourself concretely with specific action words which will arise easily if you follow my advice in this chapter.

MORE THINGS TO AVOID

Negativity; saying "I can't believe I'm doing this" or "Just trying this out".

Bad puns and stupid jokes.

Desperate Dan phrases like "Searching for Soul-mate".

Dishonesty; pretending you have a perfect body, champagne and caviar wallet or are 10 years younger than your real age. This might get you a first date, but you'll be history once your lies are exposed.

Choosing your words carefully is very different from dishonesty:

- Instead of saying "hates cooking";
  Say: "enjoys romantic candlelit evenings out".

- Instead of saying "Can't balance a check book";
  Say: "Creative hobbies like painting and photography".

When it comes to the kind of man you want:

- Instead of saying "short men need not apply";
  Say: "Tall and imposing turns me on".

- Instead of saying, "I don't suffer fools gladly so motor mechanics and artisans can go jump";
  Say: "Love reading, crosswords, theatre and classical music".

If all else fails, you can hire a professional "profile writer" from the following sites:

Profile Helper: http://www.profilehelper.com is a place where you can either have a profile written from scratch, or re-written with more flair. They will also critique your photos.

Evan Marc Katz: http://www.e-cyrano.com/ calls himself a "personal trainer for love". If you want inspiration, read a profile that Katz says won his client the man of her dreams http://www.e-cyrano .com/services.html?stories1.html

WRITE A KILLER PROFILE HEADLINE

Copywriters will tell you that an advert's success depends hugely on a brilliant headline that acts as a hook to snag immediate curiosity or interest.

Your Profile is no different.

Grab attention and make him curious, wanting to know more about you.

Then once you have aroused interest, draw him in, line by line.

THE BRAND "YOU"

Think of yourself as the **brand** "You" as Tom Peters, a leading American marketing guru, once put it. Remember the difference between *features* and *benefits* when describing a product – which, in this case, is You.

Get a pen and paper. Close your eyes. Open your heart lovingly and kindly as you think about yourself. Pretend you are sitting cozily with a good friend, describing your personal likes and dislikes. These are your *features*. Then consider the positive things that people compliment you on and like about you. These are the *benefits* of knowing, and being with, you.

MIND MAP

If you get stuck, do a mind-map to brainstorm on a page in your journal. Start with a word about yourself in the centre of a circle and radiate lines out with different topics. Use words, but also grab colored pens and get creative with drawing and sketching.

TREASURE MAP FOR LOVE

Spend time doing a Treasure Map for Love. This will not only serve as a useful jogger when writing your Dating Profile, but will also act as a powerful tool of manifestation because, once complete, it will be a constant visual reminder of your dream love life – and you'll be amazed how exact replicas of images you choose one day show up in real life.

Many years ago I did a Treasure Map for a romance book I wanted to write entitled Magic Island Love, in which I had pictures of a couple in love, with island scenery in the background. I spent months trying to write the book, but finally chucked it away in frustration – I decided I was not cut out to write romantic fiction, and would focus instead on writing nonfiction books for the body-mind-spirit genre.

But something must have stuck with me. Recently I realized with a jolt that, in terms of the Law of Attraction, I had created my own Treasure Map – I had taken the essence and deep feelings of love attached to the pictures and manifested them in my life; I'm now married to my Love Hero Nick, living on our "magic island of love", the Isle of Wight.

HOW TO CREATE YOUR LOVE TREASURE MAP

To create your Love Treasure Map, you will need:

- A good-sized piece of poster board or A3 sheet of paper;
- A stack of magazines that you can cut up – include travel, home, garden, woman's interest and any others that most reflect your interests;
- Scissors and glue; and
- Several hours of free time one afternoon or evening when you can put on some music and invite in your angels or spiritual guides to inspire you.

Flip through the magazines and tear or cut out images, words and pictures that appeal to you and make you feel good about life, your dreams or interests that you have, or would like to try one day.

Try not to *think* too hard about the pictures and words you are collecting, take a light-hearted, intuitive approach that draws on your heart and imagination. Remember this is a *Love* **Treasure Map** – so include at least one appealing picture of a couple in love, as well as other romantic images that symbolize love, commitment and joy.

When you have a large pile of pictures, assemble them into a creative collage and stick them onto your board or page. Some love coaches suggest you include a picture of yourself looking happy and fulfilled in your Love Treasure Map. But I prefer to choose pictures that represent my imagined **Future Self**, as that has always worked for me.

Look at your collage – it vividly depicts the excitement and passions of a woman who appears interesting and magnetic to men browsing her profile.

How would you describe this woman from the collage? Just start writing, and your profile will develop into someone like this: "I am a warm, sensuous woman who likes both the finer things in life as well as nature and animals. I love to cook, especially Italian food, and enjoy sharing a meal with a loving someone over a glass of wine. I grow my own herbs in my patio garden and enjoy fresh flowers in the house, especially yellow roses."

Keep writing. See how many of the senses and vivid details you can include to bring yourself to life online.

DON'T BE A PERFECTIONIST

Remember, it doesn't have to be perfect; you can add and change it whenever you like.

I went through many different versions of my own profile over the years, but here's the one that drew the most response:

WANTED: A HERO FOR MY ROMANTIC FANTASY
The Heroine

Warm, caring, intuitive; loves roses, silk sheets, scented aromatherapy oils; laughter...

Also... nature, animals, classical/melodious music, books (self-help or pacey novels like Judi Picoult or John Grisham) good movies, art, concerts, theatre.

But hold your horses... she's also very energetic, gregarious, and enjoys exercise like hiking, swimming, yoga and gym.

Compassionate and caring, this Heroine is truly an eternal optimist who daily counts her blessings and genuinely believes every dark cloud has a SILVER-GOLD lining and will ultimately bring life-enhancing rain to help her soul grow and her heart blossom!

Her kids have left home – but she lives with a friendly and lively border collie dog called Shep, who she loves to walk along the beach or in a nature reserve.

She has faced some tough challenges, but that has made her fearless and feisty in the face of change. And somewhat adventurous to travel, explore and see each day anew.

She describes her ideal match thus:

The Hero

He is kind, humorous and well-spoken! A man of integrity and strength. He is thoughtful, caring and sexy. Intelligent, tactile and... knows how to please a woman! Adventurous and... playful; faithful when he commits.

Above all, he is tired of playing the field / being alone and is now ready for a lasting, loving relationship of trust, honesty, commitment.

PART 2: YOUR WINNING PROFILE PICTURE

Not having a photo is the **single biggest mistake** you can make in your profile. Don't sabotage yourself. You can boost your chances of success 1000 percent, just by including an appealing photo of yourself with your profile.

Profiles without photos suggest you have something to hide.

And that hackneyed phrase "ask for my picture" will get you nowhere!

A picture really is worth a thousand words. So trust me and read on about some dos and don'ts with photos.

TOP TIPS FOR A WINNING PICTURE

1. Invest in a professional studio photographic session. You certainly don't trust your health, your vision or even your haircut to an amateur – so why would you trust your online image to one? Who said using a professional photographer is "cheating"? My friend who is a professional young model ended up taking my profile shots in a semi-studio setting with make-up and props. I wanted pictures I could use for my brochures and website as well and I was thrilled with the results, especially as she's also adept with photo-shop.

    Yes, I certainly looked more glamorous than usual, but it was still me in the pictures. Whatever you do, **don't** use a passport mug shot or holiday pose on a mountain top with bad lighting.

2. Don't "age shave" by posting a picture more than two or three years old. Dates feel short-changed if they meet a very much older version of the person depicted in the online profile.

3. Under no circumstances include a second or third person in your photo. From my own experience, I have found that men with their grown up daughters draped on their arms, are usually suspect in some way – like they're trumpeting "love me, love my grown-up daughter", to stave off intimacy.

4. Do not show too much skin or cleavage... at least on the over-40/50 dating sites we are discussing, with the intention of meeting a romantic soul-mate.

Most importantly – **JUST DO IT!**

TO SUM UP

In this chapter I advised you on the best ways to create a confident, magnetic profile and winning picture.

Once you've decided to dip your toe in the water, don't let the challenge of writing and posting your profile delay you from diving right in. Stick to my suggestions and you'll be giving yourself a huge advantage over the average person putting up a profile without any guidance.

Remember to line up your energy before you begin and value the time you spend creating your Love Treasure Map and Timeline images. Keep them at the forefront of your mind every day to visualize your Love Hero.

By following my advice in this chapter – your profile will both shine and have that magnetic pulling power you need for online dating success.

CHAPTER SIX:
TOP ONLINE DATING SITES & MOBILE APPS

In this chapter I will introduce you to the wealth of online dating sites available, and steer you in the right direction. The choice can seem overwhelming at first, but once you find a few sites that suit you, you will quickly become familiar with them and it will be as easy as checking your emails.

FREE OR PAID?

If you're new to online dating you may think it's best to try a *free* online dating site first – after all, you've got nothing to lose, right?

Wrong!

Paid subscription sites are less likely to have creepy or dishonest users, posting profiles or contacting you, because having to whip out a credit card and register formally acts as a screening mechanism in your favor as a genuine user. So my advice is go with a tried-and-tested site and pay at least **one months' subscription**. Later you can consider a six month investment, which will reduce your monthly subscription.

MOBILE DATING APPS

The very latest development in online dating is people searching dating sites via mobile apps on their smartphones. According to a recent study by Flurry, a world leader in mobile app analytics, there has been a huge surge since 2008 in the time people spend on their smart phones and tablets. It seems that individuals are using dating apps more rapidly than any other kind of app available, including games, news and entertainment.

Match.com and eHarmony can both be accessed by computer and an app on your Smartphone or iPad. They are my top two recommendations, partly because of their reputations, but also because they were where I spent most of my time while internet dating. They were where I felt most comfortable and got the most consistent and best results. But I have also listed several sites that cater specifically for the over-40s.

TOP ONLINE DATING SITES

MATCH.COM

Last year alone, more than 500,000 singles found meaningful relationships through Match.com's online personals and singles ads. According to Match.com the company pioneered the internet dating industry, launching in 1995.

Many say they are the most recognized dating service worldwide, and indeed they serve more than 15 million singles in 240 countries.

This isn't a specifically over 40 online dating website, but is one of the best-known and, due to the sheer numbers signed up, you will find that a good portion of the population are over 40. That said, because of its size, it is a bit hit-and-miss and often likened to a meat market.

A snazzy layout, easy-to-use search features and numerous magazines, newsletters and advice columns round out the already jam-packed Match.com site. One common complaint is that they don't show their monthly subscription fee until you sign up – it's about $30 a month.

Important advice, as with all sites, is to read the fine print – if you don't cancel formally yourself after the first month, they will continue to bill you a recurring monthly fee. So just be aware if you do sign up.

As usual, you can set up your profile and view other people for free, but if you want to contact anyone you need to be a paid-up member. The backhanded silver lining to the high monthly fee is that if you don't find someone within six months, you get the next six months free...

EHARMONY.COM

eHarmony sets itself apart from other online dating sites by offering advanced matching based on its patented **29 Dimensions® of Compatibility** for lasting and fulfilling relationships. This test was developed by its founder, Dr Nick Warren, who is a clinical psychologist and author of eight books on love, marriage and emotional health. During 35 years, counselling thousands of married couples, Dr Warren observed a set of characteristics that seemed to be present in all successful relationships. Calling them the 29 Dimensions® of Compatibility, he confirmed that these dimensions were highly predictive of relationship success and could be used to match singles.

Many people like the Guided Communication feature which helps you break the ice with someone you like the look of if you are shy. Success is shown in the thousands of long-lasting relationships that have been facilitated by the eHarmony dating site in the past 10 years. A survey shows that its compatibility matching is responsible for nearly 4% of U.S. marriages (that's 44,000 member weddings annually or 120 eHarmony weddings a day).

Clearly eHarmony's system works a treat! So if you are looking for a marriage partner, eHarmony has a better than average success rate for bringing happy couples together.

The site has a free option and a paid option – which is pretty pricey at $59.95 for one month or $19.95 per month for a 12-month subscription.

You may want to start by dipping your toe in the water with something less expensive than either Match.com or eHarmony, so here are some alternative recommendations for you to investigate.

BABYBOOMERDATES.COM

This website brings together a network of online dating sites aimed at single people over 45, although they are not strict about the age limit.

When you sign up to be a member of this parent site, you gain access to a wide range of niche sites within the same age parameters such as Military Singles, Animal Lovers and Single Parents. This means that you can hone in on someone with similar interests very quickly.

As with most sites, the free membership allows you to post a profile, view other members and "smile" at someone if you are interested in them, but if you want to do more you will need to upgrade. Paying for the membership enables you to email others and get rid of those pesky adverts.

OVER40ANDSINGLE.COM

As the advert goes: "It does what it says on the tin." If you are over 40 and single, then look no further, this is a good site for you.

What's even better about this site is that it is completely free, meaning that you can post a full profile and look for other members without having to pay for a membership. But you can also email, instant message and video chat with people you like. As if that wasn't enough, you can even get advice from some online articles targeted at 40+ somethings.

PERFECTMATCH.COM

Another website aimed specifically at the over 40s, this one boasts its own Duet® Total Compatibility System. You can use the comprehensive tool – which markets itself as one of the most reliable profile analysis programs – to search all the profiles to find your best match.

This site also offers a variety of advice articles, ranging from online dating safety to seasonal ideas and a dating checklist. You can even ask their dating expert questions if you find yourself repeatedly unlucky in finding someone.

It has won some awards and is said to deliver one of the highest user-satisfaction rates.

OVER40SONLINEDATING.CO.UK

This British site is aimed at the burgeoning over 40s singles market and is a popular, fast-growing site. Using the tag, "Life begins at forty", they are a reassuring outfit designed to make the more mature online dater feel comfortable.

You can join for free to browse other members anonymously by postcode, but you need to pay to set up your own profile, receive messages and get other benefits.

LAVALIFE.COM

This site offers three communities to meet someone with whom you can build the exact type of relationship you desire.

The Dating community is perfect if you are only after a few dates and some casual flirting, but if you are looking for something more serious then you can browse the Relationship section.

FACEBOOK

Finally, if I was to start over now (2017/2018) I would search on Facebook for pages and groups that cater to attracting love and/or online dating/older dating. Helpfully, when you click on one page or group Facebook will show you other similar pages you may find interesting. While you are there hop on over to LIKE **my** Facebook page dedicated to you here: **@attractloveonlineguide** and tell me how I can help you further!

TO SUM UP

There are a wide variety of online dating websites – and mobile dating apps – for you to choose from and the approach you take will be whatever suits you.

You can cast your net wide with one of the big name sites such as Match.com or eHarmony.com to benefit from the volume of members, while accepting that many people will be too young and it can feel like a bit of a meat market.

Alternatively, you can target the over 40s market with a number of dedicated age-related sites, or you can target your particularly hobbies or interests through specialist sites.

The key is to give it a try and find what suits you best.

CHAPTER SEVEN:
THE DOWNSIDE OF ONLINE DATING

In this chapter I reveal a dark sad secret about online dating from my own personal experiences. It's something you need to prepare yourself for so that it doesn't destroy your hopes and dreams and send you scuttling back to singledom.

I've seldom told anyone about it because I prefer to focus on the positive. But I wouldn't be doing you any favors to pretend it's all light and breezy when it comes to putting your heart and soul into online dating.

Let's face it: at some stage on your journey to find true love you will hit what John Bunyan called in Pilgrim's Progress – the Slough of Despond. And it's not a pretty place to land, believe me.

One minute you're riding high on the merry-go-round of online dating; your head is thrown back in delight, cheeks glowing, juices flowing.

Then KA-BOOM; before you know what's hit you, you've toppled, bruised and despondent, into the slush, and you didn't even see it coming.

LESSON #1
It's a numbers game.

Don't expect to be successful 100% of the time. You win some... and you lose some (or many) as time goes on.

Luck does come into it, to some extent, and we have seen how you can ramp up your chances for luck and love by transforming your thoughts, emotions and intentions.

CASE STUDY: MEETING NICK

It took me several years fishing in the online dating seas before I met my true love, Nick.

I believe we were destined to be together, but perhaps it took longer than anticipated because I had some valuable lessons to learn about myself, life and love, that make our marriage today so rich and wonderful.

While I was learning patience and how to tackle the challenges of rejection, despair and building my self-worth, he was on his own journey of healing from the grief of being widowed.

So I'm glad I stayed the course.

And you must too!

LESSON #2
Never give up.

Your longing is there for a reason and you must keep going, no matter what happens.

But don't set yourself up to be hurt for longer than necessary. What is the secret of keeping yourself from being damaged through all this?

Friends can be wonderful so long as they don't dissuade you from going back into online dating if you have a big disappointment.

Rather seek a knowledgeable and supportive counsellor or coach to help you negotiate the rapids and get over or release the intensity of the break-ups and disappointments. Naturally I highly recommend coaches like myself who use fast-acting emotional healing work like EFT and Matrix Reimprinting to clear the root cause in subconscious beliefs that keep attracting the experiences you'd rather not have!

LESSON #3
Don't take 'No' or rejection personally.

There'll come a time when you have to recognize the signs that – to quote the title of that classic book by Greg Behrendt and Liz Tuccilo - *He's Just Not That Into You!*

What do you do? Go after the guy? Lick your wounds in silence? Or just go back searching online?

Let me pull the curtain back on some of my own true dramas in online dating.

CASE STUDY

For weeks on end, the new profile pictures I put up looking and feeling flirty, gorgeous and blonde, sexy and enticing were working. Like a kid in a toyshop at Christmas, I got excited at the flow of emails pinging into my folders. Like Meg Ryan in the movie *You Got Mail*, my heart leapt at each new computer message.

He looks great – he's got a nice smile – he's just my type. Spacing a few dates each week, I took it step by step with the main contenders on the list. Obviously I graciously backed out from the non-starters.

But at the same time, I expected to strike it lucky as well. And when that didn't happen, the hungry ghosts of emotional despair came to haunt me.

I kept a smile on my face, but was crying inside.

I texted Jan, the widower who liked hiking and had been coming to my flat for late-night coffees and chats. We have been dating (but I use that word judiciously as he has shown no interest in commitment) for two months, yet I tell myself... this could be love.

His text response is non-committal – "watching a movie right now."

"What movie?" I text back, hopeful, lonely and hinting.

"Charlie and the Chocolate Factory."

Nothing more... I wait. And wait. And wait.

Then, disgusted, I switch off my cell phone and sink deeper into my slough of despond. I can drive myself crazy asking, "Is he still grieving for his wife? Is he babysitting his grandchildren?" It sounds like it from the choice of movie. Frankly I'll never know – I need to accept that "He's just not that into you."

Says Behrendt: "Let me paint you a picture of what you'll never see when you're with a guy who's really into you. You'll never see you staring maniacally at your phone, willing it to ring... You'll never see you hating yourself for calling him when you know you shouldn't have. What you will see is you being treated so well that no phone antics will be necessary. You're too busy being adored."

Time to remember that the next amazing man I encounter with the really "good excuse" I make for him when he doesn't call – is just another guy running his own agenda which I don't have to take personally or sweat over. Time to delete him from the list. And move on...

I check into my emails – there is one message.

This time it's an email from Rowan – who promised to contact me when he came into town from his retirement home on the coast. I had previously sent him a catch up email regarding an international air show he was scheduled to attend:

"Hi Rowan,

What happened to you - did the Airshow go well?

Are you still interested in meeting?"

Like a hole in the head, this lonely Saturday night, I got his reply:

"Hi Caryl,

Thanks for the mail and sorry that I haven't been in contact for a while now, but I've purposely been keeping a low profile. The long and short of it is that I met a lovely lady and I'm now fully committed to give this new relationship a chance to blossom. I really would loved to have met you. But hey, who knows what the future holds."

It's getting laughable. So I phone my platonic friend Gerry; he's sure to make me see things in perspective.

Gerry, my sales-coach friend, reminds me that for every 10 strikes in cold calling you end up with two or three hits. So the more failures I get… the better my chances of ultimate success.

There is a season for everything: a time to plant; a time to reap; a seed falling on fertile ground when it's time.

So that means the list of 'No's has to be worked through without emotional attachment or feelings of rejection. That is something diffi-cult to remember. What to do but hope your luck changes tomorrow?

Hope, as GK Chesterton said, is the power of being cheerful in circumstances that we know to be desperate. So, we reframe the situa-tion positively: at least Rowan didn't lead me on and then dump me.

LESSON #4
Move on.

Best advice from Behrendt and Tuccillo is, "Don't ask yourself what you did wrong or how you could have done it differently. Don't waste your valuable heart and mind trying to figure out why he did what he did, or thinking back on all the things he said, and wondering what was truth and what was a lie. The only thing you need to know is that it's really good news – he's gone; hallelujah!"

So dear reader, you pick yourself up, dust yourself down... and eventually, start all over again!

TO SUM UP

In this chapter I opened the trapdoor on the dark sad secret you may not want to hear – that eventually you can expect to face the suffering, rejection, despair and despondency that occur on the journey of online dating.

From my own experience I shared four lessons that add up to one simple answer: learn to recognize when he's just not that into you – but don't take it personally. Keep on – perseverance will see you succeed in the end!

CHAPTER EIGHT:
SPOTTING MEN WITH COMMITMENT-PHOBIA

"Nothing takes the taste out of peanut butter quite like unrequited love."
Charlie Brown

In this chapter you will learn to spot a commitment-phobic male in the jungle of online dating. I explain *why* it's so important, and what to do to ensure you attract the kind of partner who wants to commit his heart and life to you.

Ladies come closer. Listen carefully. This advice will save you a load of heartache and wasted tears and time.

6 WAYS TO SPOT THE MALE COMMITMENT-PHOBE

There is a species of the male variety that prowls the cyberworld as surely as in real life. I call him the **Commitment-Phobe** – i.e. he has a phobia about commitment!

From my personal experience, you can spot him by the following traits and learn to stay far away.

He hasn't been married by the time he's 50 or 60 – he may tell you he was "married to his business", and have the bucks to prove it, but trust me he's a commitment-phobe!

He's a poor-me victim who says his ex-wife took him to the cleaners while numerous business deals went belly-up – even if he says he wants to commit, steer clear because he'll never change his spots!

He has been divorced or single more than 10 to 15 years. Sorry chaps, I don't care what excuses you have, that's a long time to be foot-loose and fancy free. Admit it; you like your single status. You may be keen to link up with a lady to date in order to fix a short-term craving for attention and/or sex. But in my experience, you're the type that reveals yourself even on the first date; judging and belittling women you've dated or were married to, your mother and women in general.

He tells you that he had a mid-life crisis 20 years ago and left his wife for a much younger woman, but then ended it because she wanted to marry and have kids of her own. (True story! I had one brief en-counter with an older man who told me this – I certainly didn't want a man with such shallow values.)

He tells you his plans for the coming holiday season are to spend 10 days in a silent retreat at a Buddhist Centre far from the hustle and bustle of life. You won't change him baby, he's a loner, recluse, mystic. Bless him and move on, fast.

Unresolved mother-issues. Red alert, you'll get the projection of his unresolved anti-female feelings and a million excuses why he can't commit. Run fast.

WHY COMMITMENT IS IMPORTANT

The word "commitment" is powerful; it evokes strong reactions from hope and happiness, to resistance and fear.

Experts say you need a minimum of three ingredients to make a relationship work in the long-term… chemistry, compatibility and commitment. And trust me, I know that to be true!

Commitment is both a blessing and curse when it comes to Internet Dating and your own e-dating code.

From personal experience, I know the word is a biggy because… just when I blamed the men I was dating for being commitment-phobes, *I ended up realizing it was my own issue as well.*

It hit me like a ton of bricks one day. After many months of serial meeting-and-dating from the internet, I realized that all the men I was meeting showed an aversion to any kind of commitment, and it was driving me crazy.

Either they had been badly burned by past marriages and relationships, or they seemed happy to play the field. Some expressed a kind of horror and revulsion about women who brought up commitment early in the process of dating, as if it were a sign of clingy neediness. Others revealed how they had been badly scarred by past marriages or recent hurt; expressing the attitude of comedian Robin Williams: "Ah, yes, Divorce, from the Latin word meaning to rip out a man's genitals through his wallet." Much-married rock star Rod Stewart has also joked bitterly: "Instead of getting married again, I'm going to find a woman I don't like and just give her a house."

At first I blamed the fact that internet dating is a fabulous and obviously tempting smorgasbord of endless opportunities for men and women *not* to commit, instead just continually sampling the wares.

But there are so many success stories of couples settling down in wedded bliss that I began to question my belief. I then asked myself a searching question, "Was it possible the world (and men I attracted) was somehow mirroring my own deep-seated beliefs and attitude; *that I was in fact the biggest commitment-phobe of all?*"

BINGO!

All my life – as a child witnessing my mother's abusive treatment by my father, and for most of my own 25-year marriage – the concept of being trapped and imprisoned by marriage came through strongly.

The moment I realized that this was possibly keeping me alone and single, I felt a shift. But I also set up several appointments with an EFT expert to help me go back and clear the childhood source of my fears and beliefs still holding me hostage as an adult.

I recognized eventually that I shouldn't be too hard on myself because I was dealing with a Younger Self who set up solutions to problems she couldn't figure out any other way. I chose to be easy on myself and take it step-by-step. Only when I was absolutely sure I was ready for lasting love, could I send out my wish to the Cosmic Ordering Service and expect to have it fulfilled in a timely manner.

In the meantime, I decided to enter into a <u>fully committed relationship with myself</u>. Randy Glasbergen's cartoon of a woman in a wedding dress speaking to her friend sums it up best: "***I needed someone who would always love and adore me, always find me fascinating, someone to spoil me rotten and never leave. So I married myself!***"

It was a relief to collapse the confusing and frustrating no-win game I had been unconsciously playing. But I can tell you to wise up when you encounter the real life commitment-phobic man and run a mile!

7 QUALITIES CHECKLIST FOR A SERIOUS RELATIONSHIP

Here is my Checklist for Serious Relationship success, I recommend it for anyone ready for committed love, with the right partner:

- Commitment to personal growth;
- Commitment to me, and our relationship;
- Emotional openness and communication;
- Integrity;
- Maturity and responsibility, including financial stability;
- High self esteem;
- Positive attitude towards life.

Experts suggest you also run the following criteria past any man you are considering spending your life with… (Yes I know, if you are in your late 40s or 50s child bearing is not relevant, but it shows the kind of person you want around your own "inner child").

- Would I want to have a child with this person?
- Would I want to have a child just like this person?
- Would I want to become more like this person?
- Would I be willing to spend my life with this person if he never changed from the way he is now?

Also check for recognized long-term relationship killers such as:

- Significant age difference;
- Different social, ethnic, or educational background;
- Toxic in-laws;
- Toxic ex-spouse;
- Toxic step-children; or a
- Long-distance relationship with no chance to relocate.

FEAR FACTOR

A person who fears commitment also lives with other deep-seated **inner fears**:

- Fear of the future;
- Fear of being hurt;
- Fear of choosing the wrong person;
- Fear of turning out like the parents whose marriage no doubt ended up seeming boring, dull, sexless; drudgery without any freedom.

No matter how you look at it – without commitment your relationship will be superficial and directionless. **With commitment**, comes a new depth of love and intimacy that strengthens caring and sharing, trust and dependability.

Commitment is golden because it:

- Gives a relationship *purpose*; without commitment it's a rudderless ship, at the whim of current and breeze;

- Invests *you* in your relationship – the difference between renting vs. buying a house.

- Creates emotional and sexual safety. Monogamous sex, once you have had your HIV-AIDS all-clear test, makes sense in this day and age. They say that commitment almost doubles a woman's orgasm-meter, and I can vouch for that.

But, at the end of the day, do remember... making a commitment to the *right* person will emotionally liberate you. Making a commitment to the *wrong* person will emotionally cripple you. It must be right to feel good!

TO SUM UP

It is important to be wary of the man who is averse to commitment after you've been dating a few months. Why? Because awareness will stop you wishing, hoping and wasting your time.

First check that you are not part of the problem with your own subconscious beliefs and programs about commitment – using EFT Tapping, Matrix Reimprinting and other clearing techniques.

I have shown you how to spot signs that your long time date is not going to commit to you, but it takes a lot of courage to put the theory into practice and walk away from a relationship that is going nowhere. For your own sake, I promise you it's worth it.

CHAPTER NINE:
WEB-SPEAK MADE SIMPLE

In this chapter I will help you decode the tech terms and language of the internet and text world which may be puzzling to some of you baby boomers of 40/50+ who are not familiar with all the terms you may encounter.

Given the global nature of internet dating, (where you can meet people online from the Philippines to Philadelphia; from the Ukraine to Utah; Argentina to Athens; Cape Cod to Cape Town) it makes sense that a new universal computer/web/cellular phone language has sprung up, but it may sometimes baffle, confuse or frustrate you.

So, whatever generation you are, it may help to have the following short-list of web-speak translated.

TERMS

Google – a verb meaning to go into the Google search engine, type in a name or item you want, and hey presto, get extensive web-sites, newsgroups and news items related to your search. Google stalking is a more intrusive version of same verb. It could impress – or freak out – your new net-date so go easy with describing your tactics here.

Blog/Blogging – online journal. This mostly free and fabulous self-expression tool is also used in such endeavors as writing a "blog to book" and getting a high profile for a company CEO as part of the marketing mix.

Vlogs/Vlogging – Video blogs, posting self-made videos for fun and/or information.

ACRONYMS

ASL – A request for your Age, Sex and Location used in Chat rooms

AWYR – Awaiting Your Reply

BRB – Be right back

F2F – face-to-face

GU – Geographically Undesirable – most dating sites allow you to specify the location for your searches as some people feel it a waste of time to trawl across country or between countries, while others meet and marry across continents (like I did).

HAK – Hugs and Kisses

IRL – In Real Life; that place where people interact in the "real" world and not simply in cyber-space.

LOL – Laughing Out Loud; what you do when your net-friend and you chuckle over a shared joke online. Not advisable to put after your own jokes! Can be confused with Lots of Love.

TMI – Too Much Information; be careful you don't say too much too soon! This is not a therapy session. You don't have to reveal upfront in lurid detail that your kids are in drug rehab or that your ex ran off with your best friend. Less is best about past partner dramas... Keep it light and truthful without going into your horror stories. You may think you are being funny to describe your ex as "psychopath", but it may scare off your dates like a neon sign flashing "baggage" (see below).

BAGGAGE – a term used about any negative aspects of a new date or relationship. This can range from having kids still living at home (especially if they are over 30!) to ex-spouses who hover in the wings literally or subconsciously.

BLOCK USER – a lovely feature allowing you to block any unwanted person on a dating site from further contact.

E-DATING OR E-DUMPING – electronically generated dating and / or dumping or saying goodbye. Allegedly less painful than rejecting you F2F...

HANDLE – In internet dating, the online name or persona you choose for your profile is your "handle." In 3D or virtual reality games and in some chat forums on the Web, this is the nom de plume or display name you use to represent yourself. By extension this can become an Avatar or online icon – say a unicorn, bluebird or any creature or object that seems right. The name comes from the Hindu religion where an avatar is an incarnation of a deity; hence, an embodiment of an idea or greater reality.

EMOTICONS – emotional graphics or visual ways to express the way you feel when words alone just aren't enough.

HIDE PROFILE – A feature of some dating sites that allows you "time out" to hide from the search of hungry eyes. This usually means you have enough dates to go on with. I learned early on to juggle about 4 potentially interesting dates at once – more than that felt overwhelming. I learned by watching my attractive 30-something friend Helen getting swamped when 80 men wrote to her in her first week online and she felt beholden to email, phone and meet each of them.

NETIQUETTE – The dos and don'ts that apply specifically to the internet world of chat rooms and dating sites.

- Do... parallel date by exchanging emails with several potential partners at the same time – it is expected and acceptable, until you both agree to give your relationship a go and the next step is then "taking off your profile" to show your new love you have eyes and emails... only for him or her.
- Don't... give out your phone number or suggest meeting in your first emails.
- Don't... bad-mouth previous dates or men you've encountered in your past.
- Don't... share too much personal information at the start.

PHOTO FRAUD – Yes it happens. Sometimes blatantly, and sometimes tongue-in-cheek. It's okay to photo-shop your picture a wee bit (see how to get a winning profile), but it should still be you – just you at your best.

PLAYER – Web slang for a fraudster who is stringing you along and could be a borderline nutcase. Like the hit I got one day from someone saying he was a 35 years old gynecologist and into "fun." I blocked him immediately and used the option available on most Dating Sites to "report him" to the web-master.

EPILOGUE

Dear Reader,

I hope you have learned something of value, hope and inspiration from my own adventures in online dating and the success tips I have passed on to you.

You deserve to ditch the Love Villains – and call in, by Law of Attraction, your Love Hero.

My main message is to never lose faith in your own worth and deserving to be treated with love and respect, by any man you meet and date online (or offline for that matter).

Never give up on your vision of being in the perfect relationship – but at the same time choose to be happy with or without partner. Because when your Love Hero does eventually show up on your website – or mobile app – on his white stallion (or BMW), promise yourself that you'll never put him before your own happiness and well-being.

Tell the cosmic male ordering service that you expect love, respect, devotion and commitment from your Love Hero in a way that matches your own deserving heart.

Use EFT Tapping whenever you need to clear the emotional or energetic static which compromises your happiness – especially to ward off feelings of rejection when your emails are ignored or a promising date goes wrong.

Revisit your Love Vision Board daily and journal positive affirming scenarios about your dreamed Love Hero and how it will be when you are together.

Repeat affirmations like:

"Online dating means I never have to feel abandoned, sorry for myself or stay home alone."
"I take my power back from feeling like a victim of the past."
"I learn and grow from every situation."
"I expect the highest and the best from my adventures in online dating."

And above all remember the Moody Blues' song, *I Know You're Out there Somewhere* which I linked to at the start of this book.

Your Love Hero is out there somewhere – use these tips and tools to attract him.

Remember to contact me for a *free Breakthrough Skype or telephone session* on your personal online dating challenges. I can use my intuitive savvy and practical emotional healing tools to help you breakfree and set you up to become magnetic to your Love Hero.

Then you will – like me – settle in for happiness and true soul mate love with that Love Hero of your dreams.

The end – and hopefully your new beginning.

Blessings and much love,

Caryl Westmore

CONTACT THE AUTHOR

Caryl Westmore is a Goal Success EFT Love Coach and expert trainer in energy psychology tools, EFT tapping (Emotional Freedom Techniques), Matrix Reimprinting and the Law of Attraction.

Feeling inspired and ready to take action?

Contact Caryl for a FREE one-hour *Break Free to Attract Your Soul Mate Now!* Laser Coaching session by phone or Skype in which she will shine a light on clearing the blocks to attracting your Love Hero and lasting true love into your life.

Email her now: cwestmoreyes@gmail.com or Skype: **breakfreefast**

Made in the USA
San Bernardino, CA
23 January 2020

63544376R00053